Wakefield Press

WomanSpeak

Woman Speak

LOUISE NICHOLAS
and JUDE AQUILINA

Wakefield
Press

Wakefield Press
16 Rose Street
Mile End
South Australia 5031
www.wakefieldpress.com.au

First published 2009
This edition published 2022
Reprinted 2026

Designed and typeset by Clinton Ellicott, Wakefield Press

ISBN 978 1 86254 847 3

A catalogue record for this book is available from the National Library of Australia

Contents

Foreword

I first met Jude and Louise about 5 years ago, when we shared the podium for education of professionals for Women's Health. Already, I knew their 'edu-poem' about the mammogram from the back of the women's toilet door. Their serious aim, to make women aware of health issues by popular poetry, is fantastic and must be applauded and encouraged. They have made an art form of attending lectures about health issues and then re-interpreting them in a popular format. I am privileged to have been their muse – and delighted to support this collection of their works, showing all aspects of issues dear to women's hearts, minds and experiences. Women everywhere can relate to all the topics covered in this wonderful collection by two enthusiastic and gifted South Australian women.

Associate Professor Margaret Davy AM,
Director Gynaecological Oncology,
Royal Adelaide Hospital.

Preface

This book is the result of our shared love of poetry – reading it, writing it and performing it. We had known and enjoyed each other's work for several years before we realised that among our variant thoughts and concerns, we shared an interest in expressing, often in a humorous way, topics and feelings that are within the general experience of women everywhere: Jude's previous collections had included poems about women's bodies and Louise had published several humorous chapbooks on women's health procedures.

We decided to combine our skills and with the aid of an Arts SA grant, were able to expand our repertoire. As *WomanSpeak*, we were invited to perform at women's workshops and other community gatherings. We were especially pleased to be invited to read for SA Cervix Screening and at other medical conferences, as we both believe in the power of poetry to express thoughts and feelings that are otherwise inexpressible. We take a light-hearted look at some of the medical interventions that women undergo in the name of their health. Necessary they most certainly are, but comfortable and uplifting they most assuredly are not!

Each time we are invited to read, particularly the humorous poems, we are asked for copies of our poems; this book is the result of that request. However, also included in this collection are many, more reflective poems, the kind that ponder both the pleasure and the pain of what it is to be a woman . . . or a man come to that, since we have no wish to claim exclusive rights to the things we all share as thinking feeling human beings in these most difficult, yet hopeful, of times.

On the *WomanSpeak* journey we've met wonderful people: nurses, doctors, surgeons, even Australian of the Year, Professor Ian Frazer, but best of all we have met many women who have shared their stories with us, on topics from smear tests to wardrobe malfunctions. We hope you enjoy reading *WomanSpeak* as much as we enjoyed writing it.

Louise and Jude

for our daughters, Zoe and Jasmine

Ghazal of the darkness

A small girl on the verandah, and Venus grew
the longer I sat, pulsing there in the darkness.

I'd take great gulps of its magical light
as the arguing voices of adults bled into the darkness.

Secret sounds of leaves and whispers of webs,
sweet hints of fear, attuned me in the darkness.

The night garden spoke of things the sun
could never learn, in tongues of velvety darkness.

The moon was an ice cube floating high. The froth
of the milky way streaking the lip of darkness.

On nights like these I gathered voltage from the sky,
thought-naked in a bath of stars and darkness.

The photograph 1

Manly Ferry, Sydney 1909

Just beyond the deferential dip of my grandfather's head,
his first floundering on the thin ice of my grandmother's eyes,
just out of sight, around the corner, to the left, to the right,
of the blur that is her hand reaching out to his,
a gene pool is waiting to gather.

And if you hold your breath long enough,
if you become the salted wound
between one cry of a gull's heart and the next,
if you hold a magnifying glass between the sun,
as symbol of millennia past and future,
and this involuntary blink of an eye before you now,
there'll be in this image,
in the pinpoint of light before the flame,
the slow process of our becoming:

my mother, myself, my daughter, her daughter,
all of us and more,
crowding onto the deck of the Manly Ferry
at this precise moment of their first meeting.

Ultrasound

Belly-heavy, bladder lapping at the edge of sudden rain,
the pregnant woman is hoisted onto the table
to lie beneath a battery of stars.
She needs no proof the world is round;
she carries it in miniature,
feels it tumble-turn through space,
sees its disquiet, each continental drift,
in seismic undulations of her flesh.
She encircles it with her arms,
fingertips touching, restoring peace.

Now the technician anoints her with oil,
goes mountain climbing in Tibet,
skis the slopes of St Moritz,
maps the meandering course of rivers,
the dark and mysterious Limpopo
stretching from navel to pubis.
He descends to the sanctum sanctorum,
sounds its depths for signs of life:
here, moving with the languidness of fish,
the thin-limbed body;
there, the eyes shut tight against un-named shadows;
and here, the heart, the holiest of holies.

She trusts the miraculous division of cells,
the relentless ripening; feels no need to check
the requisite number of fingers and toes.
Scans the screen instead for the trace of a smile,
a flicker of recognition.
Hears again the heart,
each sonic beat like a deep-sea diver,
fists full of Spanish gold.

Fertility rites

If only the couple
desperate for a child,
their bedside a litter
of centimetre squares,
a silver-veined stamen
schlucked under her tongue
before the cock
can crow each day,
slow seep of albumen
from the cracked purse
of her eggs
precipitating
the sloughing off
of jeans and knickers
and sudden drop
to coitus don't interruptus
anywhere
anytime,
and immediate hoick
of hips overhead
(isn't it lucky
it's not salmon
she's nurturing?)

could take their eyes
off the prize
and laugh.

Third trimester

At thirty-two weeks she resembles
a giant melon, minus the barrow beneath.
Her tight belly is a map of silver rivulets.
Her legs splay out like an old dog's.
Hands on hips, she waddles to the bathroom,
tackles the stairs with the gait of the aged.
She no longer attends family dinners
where svelte sisters-in-law offer advice.

Her inner furnace rages.
She seeks a bedroom, flicks off
her damp tent-dress and bra
to lie full-frontal by a window.
Rising, she thinks of upturned beetles.
She snaps and naps at odd moments.
She hasn't seen her feet for weeks
and the mirror announces her navel has gone.

A pang makes her want to wind back time,
return to the store and tell them this body doesn't fit
but a stirring inside her, and she strokes
the stretched orb as if it were an egg.
She whispers promises to keep it warm
and she thinks about the flood
that will split her like an autumn fruit.
With big stitches and determination
she knits a first crooked bootee.

Amnion

Sometimes this beach
makes her feel hollow.
On winter days grey waves
swirl in minor chords
and the cry of a gull
seems enough to drown her.

Today, a ray of sun
on fresh pink seaweed
and the season's first
spotted cowry launch her
on a kick-board to childhood,
to rock pools of wonder.

She removes her watch,
her shirt, her jeans,
and kneels
in the shallows
like a creature
returning to the womb.

The call

Let's go down to the beach
they say in every coastal town.
Cars cruise toward magnetic sand,
where short skirts walk invisible dogs
and horns honk pheromones into the dusk.
A subliminal summer undertow
helps lovers dare deeper water.
Walking the white edge
or dancing beside a beach fire
they succumb to the sea-drug,
the sunset pre-med.

Even in grey months
young bucks strut the promenade.
The chill winds fuel their chests,
make their lips sting for the salt of a kiss.
And the thrill of a moonlit stroll,
silver waves surging
to a track through sand dunes
and a spot where salt bush forms a soft raft.

Nipples

Nipples are not on-off buttons
they are radio dials
waiting to be tuned in.
Nipples are not raisins
they are glace cherries
on frosted cup-cakes.
Nipples are not freckles
they are beauty spots
on powdered cheeks.
Nipples are not beans
they are chocolate stars,
caramel buds, aniseed rings.
Nipples are not pebbles
they are lustrous pearls
glistening in the shower.
Nipples are not shy
they are brave sherpas
leading women on journeys.

Our short love

I visit this site from time to time
via wheat field or old photograph.
You were six feet two,
forking hay into a trailer;
your shoulders were dusty, sweaty
your teeth white.

You were a loyal farmer's son.
I regret the nuzzles I pushed away,
the kisses I didn't return.
I've forgotten the sound of your voice,
the colour of your eyes.
Like the unmarked grave
of an old pet – our short love.

You asked me to be friends, to walk
with you down the main street.
You fixed my front gate
and the backyard swing.
You only did low gear.
Reliable as the seasons,
you cruised from breakfast
to dinner to breakfast again.

One day I watched you
blow away like tumbleweed
back to your dirt and seeds.

Beauty and the breast

Incarcerated behind whale-bones and wires, breasts have been raised, lowered, squashed and plied. Twenties titties were flattened into boyish fashions, but busts went forth in the forties with the conical armoured bra – the double pointed tasty-toaster which threatened those who dared dance close.

Under loose cheese-cloth, sixties breasts swung free with the sunshine and love, while the grid-iron eighties saw shoulder-pads and professional breasts under silk shirts. Bust-lines pushed up in the nineties and pumped up thereafter. Now breasts are legal tender. Surgeons get rich from them. Women sell them on glossy pages.

Yet most breasts are reclusive and look forward to their evening release. Like all twins, no two are exactly alike: the shy nipple, the small freckle, go unnoticed until a lover, like a cartographer, tongues contour lines and makes up for all those years in brassiere prison.

Vulva speak

Doctors address me as Introitus or Pudendum.
In the vernacular, I've been called
a thousand cute and furry, gross and
hairy, nicknames. I am none of these.
I know I speak for my sisters when I say
we are like any other part of the body:
as the eyes we weep in pleasure;
as the ears we respond to tempo;
as the lips we are first to kiss new life.
And as the spirit, we are martyrs –
we bleed and we tear
for the sake of mankind.

Phat is fat, however it's spelled

In this era of fat-phobia
we must not be chunky,
chubby, curvy or cuddly
– those are the better names.

And then there's: thunder thighs, jelly-belly,
tub-o-lard, and blubber-guts
to name but some.

Compared with the meagre few for thin:
skinny, lean, wiry. Where are the animal analogies,
the food references? You don't call someone
celery guts or beached garfish.
Only cutesy things like Peggy or Twiggy.

Bring in a fat tax, the fit rich say.
What about a danger tax on protruding bones?

Ah, let them eat like mice. No. Even mice eat cheese.
Leave the double-brie for those who can appreciate it most.
The fat laugh eighty percent more than the thin,
their mouths are accustomed to exercise.

While the dieters, those tight-lipped pretzels
sit glamorously, tummies tucked in
so all can savour their fancy wrappers.

Are they too tight inside? Afraid to swallow
the cocktail, to enjoy the cake, the plastic icing
and the man on top?

Roll-ons

If wearing a girdle was like enduring torture
then the roll-on was mere solitary confinement.
No bones, just a gut-displacing tube of shiny
elastic with a little bow at the top to mark
the suffocated belly-button. Sixties ladies
with Spandex attire and pointy silhouettes
modelled roll-ons for newspapers. Before
and after sketches suggested a vacuum.
Where else could the flesh have gone?
My thrifty mother filleted her corsets
but they weren't the same, things sagged
in the wrong spots. So she turned
to roll-ons, bouncing into them
when she gained weight: the little roll
of her spare tyre sat pert above her belt.

Pantyhose

In poorer times my mother cut laddered legs
from pantyhose, wore two good legs
with double tops. *A cotton gusset is a must,*
she'd claim, *so your private-parts can breathe*
and your feet don't swell.
Most modern women stand by pantyhose:
silky, sheer, easy to wear – no more
suspender belts with tricky little clips
to come undone and whip you on the legs.

Many lovers lamented the demise of stockings:
those French-maid legs parted,
the lacy Mount of Venus welcoming the canny climber.
This passage was barred when pantyhose closed
loose borders with impenetrable gussets.
And as an end note: it's a fallacy that a fart
will travel down one leg as a bulge in pantyhose –
it actually flattens and spreads
and warms your seat on a winter's night.

Delta nightclub

When the gin sets in and the
cruisers cruise, she imagines
she is swimming not dancing.
All around her: bright fabrics,
glistening skin under aquarium lights.

She knows these dark waters,
knows the great white who aims
his teeth at any new blood; the jelly fish
who feels you up on the dance floor;
and the seagull who drinks your wine
while you're gone. She knows to avoid
the school of minnows with teenage beards.

She loves this club beside the pier
where strangers make imaginary love.
And when the music stops pumping
and the lights come on, she knows
from experience how they leave
in pairs to spawn upstream.

If

If, from the back of the crowded Henley line,
my book neglected, closed upon my knee,
among the people boarding I should see
you – the ice-flow eyes, the serpentine
curl of lip, your body's muscled shrine
where I, like all your wide-eyed devotees
once worshipped till you, despite my earnest pleas,
chose to defy my newfound feminist line,

I'd wait till you were near, then turn my head,
calmly appraise that body, those lips, that face,
then smiling a smile benign and quite relaxed,
(unlike our lusty romps upon your bed)
I'd take my book, flick through to find my place . . .
wish I'd lost weight. Curled my hair. Waxed.

Aerobics

Don't make me go to aerobics Sharlene,
I tried it once before.
I didn't like it and it didn't like me,
who needs another chore?

Lycra looks shocking on my build and size,
and someone should tell the supplier
we'll all be shaving our eyebrows next
if legs are cut much higher.

It's not that I never exercise,
I do – but in my own way.
I wrestle my conscience daily in fact . . .
well . . . almost every day.

Wal used to raise my heart rate a bit
in the time-honoured way with sex.
But a sneeze beats an orgasm any day
and it saves on Codeine and Bex.

And then there's that teacher, Belinda:
Knees up, once again, double time!
Hasn't she heard of a good lie in bed?
And is chocolate the ultimate crime?

And some of the things she gets you to do
I reckon are slightly sus –
lying on your back with your knees apart –
but none of us made a fuss . . .

There you are with your head through your knees –
What if you snapped them shut?
You'd be in a right-royal pickle my dear,
with your nose sort of jammed in a rut.

I know we have to look after ourselves,
that a check-up's an absolute must.
But really Sharlene, who'd want to be
their own gynaecolo-just?

No Sharl love, you can count me out.
I won't even come for a look.
I'm flat out jogging my memory right now –
Where in the hell is that book?

The mammogram

Well Sharlene, I did it, pet. I took my lumpy breasts
and lumbered them off to that clinic of yours
for one of those awful tests.
I wish they'd find a better way . . . yes, I know that's silly.
But they would if we were blokes, Sharlene,
and we had a 'lumpy willy'?

I thought I'd try some training first, decided the thing to do
was to simulate a mammogram
so it wouldn't be anything new.
The fridge door proved successful, at least for the vertical view,
but squashing each breast horizontally
wasn't as easy to do.

The old chest freezer, so aptly named, I thought might be the thing,
but my nipples got stuck to the build up of ice
so I gave the plumber a ring.
When he came up with a couple of things he thought we might try next,
I checked his customers' service guide
and they didn't appear in the text.

But he told me about a bloke he knew – a poet, I think, or singer
who wrote about his dear old gran
whose breasts got caught in the wringer.
I could try that, I said to myself, but never mind someone's old nanna –
I remember a poem as well
called 'Coralie Sits on the Scanner'.

She wanted to thrill her boyfriend you see, by sending a saucy email:
took off her knickers, plonked herself down,
and sent it straight to his in-mail.
But he was miffed and said to his mates, 'I've given her lots of leeway,
so why would she send me this horrible shot
of something she's squashed on the freeway?'

We don't have any scanners at work but the copier did the trick.
O'course being the busy place it is
I had to be awfully quick:
I reached up under my jumper and discreetly got one out,
plopped it down, slammed the lid,
and hoped I didn't pass out.

I did that several times each side, then rushed off to the phone
and made that appointment right away
before my nerve had flown.
And there I was, the very next week, trying hard to look chaste,
my bra tucked away in my handbag
and my breasts hanging down to my waist.

Not a pretty sight I'm afraid to say as I sat there waiting my turn,
(a full-length mirror an arm's length away)
thinking of bras I'd burned.
Remember the test of a perky breast: a coin beneath one would fall?
Never mind one, try ten, try a ton,
I could hide the crown jewels and all.

But the mammogram was a piece of cake, no trouble or pain at all
since breasts with no elasticity
have no choice but to fall
and spread out flat of their own accord – like batter on a griddle.
I could almost hear them sizzling, Sharl,
the cherry adrift in the middle.

The technician stood there, hands on her hips, there was nothing much to do,
other than laugh 'cos with all I'd done
they did look a bit black and blue.
Anyway Sharl, the results were good, so what *if* that pair of lay-abouts
beat a retreat clear down to my feet?
As long as they actually stay about.

And all that training wasn't in vain – for a couple of days or more
they were shapely breasts, if I say it myself
and that plumber agrees and all.
He also says if it's inevitable, why would anyone fight it?
And if that's not in his service book,
I might just help him write it!

Fanny flashing from a feminist focus

Well Sharlene, I've found it at last. It pays to be persistent.
The perfect job for a girl like me – a Gynae Training Assistant.
A GTA to those in the know, a very important position.
I help to train young medicos, Sharl. It's given me purpose, a mission.

Of course I'm qualified – der Sharlene . . . Hang on! Come down a peg!
It's hardly open-heart my girl, it's more like . . . 'open legs'.
Smear tests, Sharl, you've heard of those? They practise first you see.
I'm always happiest flat on my back so it might as well be me.

Using a speculum's tricky, Sharl, like inserting the bill of a duck
where no duck's ever been before – it calls for more than luck.
Best not trap the odd pubic hair – has that ever happened to you?
There's a lot to be said for a triple-x wax . . . but pinching's painful too.

And getting in's not the only concern – it's a kiddies' maze in there.
Someone has to lead the way so they don't end up elsewhere.
I guess I'm a sort of tour guide, Sharl – some do the Great Wall of China.
But only the best are stationed, like me, in Deepest Darkest Vagina!

One bloke seemed to be fossicking; a miner's light strapped to his head,
peering and prodding and poking around. 'Found any gold?' I said.
And another had no idea at all. I'm legs-apart, on display:
'That's a nasty gash, I'll stitch it,' he said, and fainted dead away.

We're Fanny Flashers to some of them but I don't think that's funny.
As if it's titillation we want and a bit of extra money.
I don't, my dear, I'll tell you straight – I'm over that for good.
I wage war against cancer, Sharl, and all for the Sisterhood!

The smear test

I lie on a cold and creaking bench, awaiting the
annual smear.
I pray my modesty's covered by sheets. Alas, it
doesn't come near.
I cast my eyes to the floor below and my heart
begins to leap:
my beloved full-brief cottontails are there,
alone now in a heap.
How I wish we could be together again, how I
miss their expansive size
from the place where once my waist used to be,
to the tops of my quivering thighs.
I clasp my clammy hands together and lay them
across my chest
to protect what's quietly gone for cover – in my
armpits – my breasts.
I ask myself, is it easier for those with bodies
intact –
all perky breasts and silken thighs where mine
just over-react?
And do they, I dare to ponder anew, have similar
fears of smell?
So much, in fact, they're red and raw from
washing their bits too well?

And when they draw their knees up high and
 spread them wide apart,
do they focus their minds on matters at hand or
 on the fear they'll fart?
No doubt men too have problems 'down there',
 but resist the urge to mock it:
if something's amiss they can check it out by
 thrusting a hand in a pocket.

Mrs Pap

When it's time to take that test again – your knickers are in your shoe,
your knees are up, you're short on shame, you shudder to think of the view –
and you notice that even the ceiling here is sporting a sizeable crack,
give Polyfilla a thought or two, and another to poor Mrs Pap.

Dear Mary Papanicolaou – what a great and grave disservice
if she doesn't become and ever remain the Patron Saint of the Cervix.
For while Dr Pap invented the smear (he was clever, caring and canny)
he couldn't have done it without his wife since she supplied the fanny.

No doubt while washing the dishes one day, she got the sudden alert
that someone armed with a pop-stick and torch was busy beneath her skirt.
She lifted her hem and saw him there, then not being one to disgorge
a torrent of total dismay, enquired, 'Lose something up there George?'

Later while hanging the washing out, George was between her legs.
'There's something you need to know,' she said. 'That's not where I keep
    the pegs.'
And then when playing tennis with friends, Mary was quite distracted
when after a heavily landed lob, he had to be extracted.

He called it her 'secret garden' once, though it was a secret no more.
He'd already cut the shrubbery back and tried to prop open the door
with a range of household objects while he took a quick look around.
Sometimes he took a cutting or two from the pretty pink cells he found.

Often the entrance closed up tight no matter what he tried:
her sock darner, a spring from their bed . . . once, he got locked inside.
She drew the line at the barbecue tongs and when they lost the shoe-horn
he scuttled out to the backyard shed . . . and the speculum was born.

The rest, as they say, is history, and yet, our poor Mrs Pap
has never been honoured with accolades, not a hip-hip-hooray or a clap.
And she vanished, you know, soon after that – just took off out the gate,
with the parting words, 'Forget it George. I don't even have a prostate!'

Waiting room

We who sit with leaking bladders (prolapse pending)
know the rules of waiting room decorum.
We would no more speak than turn our heads
to left or right for fear of catching someone's eye.

So we feel a sort of schoolboy-soaring,
when a woman of no fixed complaint
takes the not insubstantial risk
of turning to the gammy leg beside her to announce

that her son, aged 35, is marrying at last,
in a tent to better accommodate his dog,
which, in its capacity as best man,
is bound to be nervous.

We strain our middle ear infections (abscess pending)
to pick up every thread of the waistcoat she's embroidering
and wonder if it's for her son or the dog
(her syntax being no help in the matter)

till the secret pocket for the rings
in a blind seam
behind his left front paw
leaves scant room for doubt.

And despite arterial blockage (infarct pending)
our hearts find room for this long-suffering woman.
Some take up the cause of incontinent dogs and blind seams
(and we all have grave concerns for the celebrant's leg).

And if our noses weren't already pressed
to the air-brushed antics
of Hollywood's latest tartlet, we might take a turn
in the rarefied air of conviviality. Or even,

since the sun has just burst through an unprotected window
and the sky has turned an unconscionable shade of blue,
force the corners of our mouths
into a pretty good imitation of a smile.

To launch into an inexplicable feeling of joy right now,
given the uncontrollable shaking of some
and the aching cheekbones of others,
would, of course, be out of the question.

Stone shoes

A quiet child, left alone to read, make craft pictures from seeds, or drip candle wax onto fingertips. I'd gorge myself on horror stories and mixed lollies; take long bike rides to look into other people's lives. Yet my feet and nostrils shied at a certain farm. *We can't go home without seeing uncle and aunt*, mother would say. The animals there wore sad, dirty faces and their water was always green; carcasses hung in the killing shed where blowflies ruled the air. I sat close to mother in the oily kitchen. *Go and play*, auntie would say. *Mind the dogs.* I didn't care to see weeping-eyed cats, or rooster feet scattered around the stump, or the pigs that drank pig-blood as uncle burnt the hair from a dripping rump. My shoes stayed weighted by my mother's skirt. And time blew the farm away.

Coffin Bay

1959

On the day our parents went out in the boat and didn't come back,
we walked along the shaded path where the tiny eyelets of light
from overhanging trees were all I knew of enchantment then
and all I know now. And when we came to the shop, we bought
blue iceblocks in square cones and sucked the sweetness
to the backs of our throats where hard lumps of fear
had risen like gelatine in homemade ice cream.

Then we walked along the water's edge as if it were the edge
of our lives, and gazed out to sea and thought of killer whales
that drape themselves in seaweed and lie in wait for stray seals,
then take them in their mouths and toss them and bat them
from one end of the bay to the other until they're tenderised
and ready for eating – except for one, which they ferry back to shore
and place gently on the sand.

And we thought of those seals and willed that our parents
would be among the chosen; that the changing tides that took them
would change again, and ferry them back to shore,
and lay them at our feet. Then out in the bay a boat appeared,
with three smaller boats trailing along behind. And in the last of them
were our parents, our mother sitting in the stern as still and serene
as the figurehead from a long-lost ship.

And we ran along the beach and skimmed a few stones
and got home in time for tea.

Prima donna

Once on a rocky beach at Tulka
I crouched beside a sea anemone
and looked and looked into that one dark eye
as though all things came from this
and begged that I might stay twelve years old forever
and not die as my sister said I would
by the slow seep of blood from secret lips.

I promised to go straight to sleep at night
and not rock and rock till the fruit
from the garden of good and evil
spilled from the corners of my mouth
if only I might be granted this one thing.

But it batted its prima donna lashes
with each ovation from the tide
and as the sun came down
in a tell-tale flush of colour
left me there to die.

The Head Mistress's speech

As the school social approaches
it is timely to remind you girls:

No minis, no denim, no platforms.
No gaudy eye make-up or spidery lashes.
No see-through fabrics. No strapless dresses.
We are not living in Caligula's time.

No G strings. No briefs.
No patent leather shoes
or the boys will see the reflection
from under your dress.

No liquor. No cigarettes.
No close dancing.
Remember, an elbow's
length apart. I will be checking.

And don't let me see you hanging about
giggling all night in the Powder Room.
You must dance.
We have taught you all the steps.

Fungi

1.

Like proud flesh on a wound of earth
the edible *phalloides*
twists its hooded stalk upward.
Silky, spongy, it rises above a leafy bed,
glistens ghostly-white
like the first penis
a girl sees in the dim light of a drive-in.

2.

Behind tall buildings, the stinkhorn,
phallus duplicatus, pops up.
Grey-skinned knobs
lurk in rings under stairways,
omit offensive odours, solicit blowflies;
repulsive as the first uninvited phallus
thrust into a young girl's view.

Peach flesh

My mother told me I would blossom one day,
take my place beside my sister who, even then,
standing on the cement stage above the septic tank,
right foot *tendu devant*, a flounce of white tulle about her hips,
reduced the flowering peach to back-drop.
Her smile was dazzle enough for the dullest of days,
her blue-black hair an even match for night.

Five years later, she would sit on a tartan rug
beneath the peach tree, the full bloom of her body
encircled in the arms of young love,
while I, beneath porch light and basin cut,
bent down, and peering through thick lenses,
scraped peach flesh from between my pudgy toes
and wondered if spring would ever come.

Plain

And when you came home from your first date with your dress undone and your glasses fogged up your mother only said *Did you have a nice time dear?* and fussed that the zipper never did sit flat as though she knew that your nights of fumbling in the back seat of a car parked four doors down of breasts plopping over-ripe into sweaty palms and the taste of someone else's tongue in your mouth pink like orthodontic alginate would be rare as acne on a beauty queen and the closest you'd come to True Love whereas your sister she of the circlet waist and hair the colour of midnight was ordered in from one more kiss under 40 watts on the front verandah every Saturday night for five years because she had something worth protecting worth preserving for the happy ever after in the third act.

At the drive-in

Everyone at the drive-in tonight
Is snogging except for you.
Trevor's engrossed in the car-chase –
What's a girl to do?
You sigh and go to the Tuck Shop
(He hardly sees you go)
But on the way back you lose your way . . .
How does anyone know
One souped-up car from another?
They're all the same to you.
But when you find it, what a surprise –
It seems he loves you too!
He opens his arms and holds you close,
His lips are seeking yours,
And then at last (oh what bliss)
An hour without a pause!
'Oh darling!' you say, 'Oh Jill!' says he,
'Be mine forever and ever.'
Which would be good but you're not Jill
And he worse luck's not Trevor.

On falling out of the car on the way home from the teachers' ball

It wasn't the tear in her new dress that hurt:
even lying semi-conscious in the gutter
the thin slice of brain that deals in practicalities
offered up her mother, the seamstress.

Nor was it the contact lens she lost when she fell:
what use are contact lenses
when your eyes have drawn the blinds
in violent shades of purple and blue?

It wasn't even the torn and bleeding flesh
of her face which, when first she saw it,
induced such moaning and invoking of heavenly hosts
her flat mate in the next room

thought she must have forgiven her boyfriend his indiscretions
and they were making up in time-honoured, multiple fashion.
It was the not knowing there was anything to make up,
and the hundred yards it took him to stop,

and her mother
looking up from the sewing machine,
her mouth a minefield of pins, saying,
'Did you fall – or were you pushed?'

Sister

My sister bears scars of arguments we had,
my nails drove into her flesh like a knife.

She went under the knife again last year,
gave her son a kidney, gave him his life.

He runs now, wins medals,
places them round her neck, says,

'I couldn't have done it without you Mum.'
Gold on gold. And who can argue with that?

The photograph 2

Manly Ferry, Sydney 1909

Again I take it down from the shelf, wander among
the passengers until I reach my grandparents,
ponder the chances of a Box Brownie opening and shutting
its one good eye at the exact moment of their meeting.

I lift my gaze to the top right corner and see for the first time
a white boat. On it are two small figures.
They are practiced in the art of sailing:
one has his hand on the tiller as though he woke
one morning and found it growing there, and now
it's so much part of his critical mass,
tiller and hand work together, like conjoined twins.
The other man adjusts the sail as if it were as commonplace
as untangling bed sheets on a good drying day.
Even the dinghy trails dutifully behind
as though it knows the ropes.

They don't realise that all those drowned in boating accidents
are lying just a freak wave or a slip of the foot away,
white-faced and waxy beneath the wrinkled skin of the sea.
They can't hear the chalky bones of countless fingers
scraping along the bottom of the boat,
the siren cries of silent mouths
the promise of eternal wisdom.

So pleased are they to be on the harbour again –
the little boat racing a wisp of cloud across the water,
dinghy yapping at its heels, sail sucking in the morning air –
they haven't noticed the ferry, let alone my grandparents:
he, in a show of striped socks and cricket whites,
she, already smitten, hand and heart outstretched.

Family tree

Our mother was always one of us, part of the circle.
Aside from the odd sexual experiment
or shaming indiscretion, we kept nothing from her.
She sobered us up, bailed us out,
dressed us down only rarely.
But on this, her eighty-sixth birthday,
our circle has become pear-shaped.
Our mother sits at the stem,
apart from its burgeoning flesh.

It's as though she's returning to the tree,
to stake her claim beside her sister.
Her parents are on the sheltering bough above;
she'll save a place for her brother,
tag it with her handbag, just in case.

If the apple doesn't fall far from the tree,
what of the pear? Thin skinned,
more easily bruised, we can't let go.
We look up at her, try to draw her back.
Gather up the photographs of holidays in Vietnam,
switch our conversation to memories of childhood –
potato printing the cubby house walls,
Sunday walks past Elephant Rock,
holidays in Coffin Bay.

She leans forward as though to speak,
adjust some detail of which she was always keeper.
Smoothes her stocking, checks that her hand-bag
is still beside her, sits back in her chair.
Her synapses have long been struggling
to keep pace with passing time.
Now they fizzle like a cooking pot plunged in cold water.

Light begins to seep from the sky;
the air grows cold.
Our mother looks round for her stick,
takes up her bag.
'It must be time to go,' she says.
Somewhere, a pear falls;
nestles into the long grass at the foot of the tree.

My mother's second husband

My mother sits enveloped in a green chair.
She's puzzling over something new.
How many times have I been married? she asks.
Only once Mum, I say.
Unless there's something you haven't told us.
She gives me that look, the one thing she can still find,
the look reserved for impertinent children.
So there isn't another man then?
And two young children?
No Mum, I say.
She slips back inside, pulls the lid down after her.
A minute later, emerges again.
I'm glad, she says.
He wasn't a nice man. He hurt the children.
He threatened to take them away.

I walk out into the sunshine.
Divest myself of aching feet and last week's rent increase.
Hold out my hands for two small children,
one on either side.

Weekly battle

After great protest, flailing arms, resistance
verbal and physical, she sits naked on the
plastic pedestal: a child's skeleton
fleshed with tissue-thin skin, wrinkled
breasts, scaly knees, all there for me to see,
and she's meek now, knows I've won.

I run the warm flannel under folds and flaps,
between bony legs then shampoo her hair
spun like a silver web on her dripping scalp.
A towel goes thrice around her frame.
She regains strength enough to complain
that this drenching will be the death of her.

She can feel the chill settling
on her chest, she says, as she shakes
her head resolved, till a dusting of talc
tickles her and raises a little giggle.
A petticoat and floral frock, rose brooch
and smile make the battle worthwhile.

Power of attorney

Her first-born son
calculates undertaker's fees,
daydreams the catalogue colours
of Mercedes Benz. He's the one
who put her in this crowded aviary
of trapped wings.

He waits like a handsome thief,
has breakfast with her,
slices the head off her egg.
He always knew how to make her dance
on the rusty tacks of her conscience –
how to make her hold a rose between her teeth
while he rifled her purse.

Now, a lawyer and a witness
in white uniform watch
as the wavering blue ink
mimics the veins on her hand.
He's quick to perch her back on her bed,
and return to the silver city
for lunch with his financial adviser.

Grandmothers

for Nell

wear beads, brooches, and feed the birds,
pin their hair into neat little rolls,
drive small dinted cars, slowly,
or walk old dogs in mid-morning parks.
Grandmothers knit on buses,
talk to children and men with pushers,
fossick at craft and fabric sales,
are frequently found in bingo halls.
They always carry safety pins, hankies;
and are known to prescribe brandy
for any ache or tingle. Some like a nip
of evening sherry to warm their cockles.
Some paint. Some write. Others wait
like fairytale princesses in cotton-wool,
white locks flowing over bony shoulders,
for the prince of release to arrive.

Loss

Not *losing*, with its
contemporaneous
possibility of turn around,
one's head, heart, senses restored.

Not *lost*, its final 't'
a missive from the front line,
its message an irretrievable plosive
with no return address.

Loss: lying in a hospital bed
to stem the flow of threatened miscarriage.
Every fifteen minutes, the nurse inquiring:
How's your *loss* going dear?
As though it might be measured,
improved upon,
bigger, better, brighter.

Until it's the mother of all losses.

Visiting the room

Evening nears. Thick elm branches
form a bridge across the last river of light.
High up in the nursery, she sits alone,
hears the soft thud of her heart, watches
a baby pink afterglow blush the clouds.
She comes here to remember, and to forget.
Her wrinkled hands smooth a pin-tuck.
The small bed creaks as she leans into
the scent of lavender. The cold makes her
hug her knees. She's careful not to crease
the satin spread as she rocks, silent.

Spidery twigs of elm pattern the dusk
like the veins in tiny wrists. Not a breath
of movement in the black leaves.
If she were to stay here long enough
if she were to hum that lullaby, and if
she stared into those scented drawers,
the room would consume her, carry her
like a burning ember above the past.
In the corner, an empty cot with rungs like bones.
She knows she must rise, for in this light
the bunny rug seems to move up and down.
She is one small step from flight,
the ledge, the little window sill,
the twisted lavender bush below
with its purple spears ready.

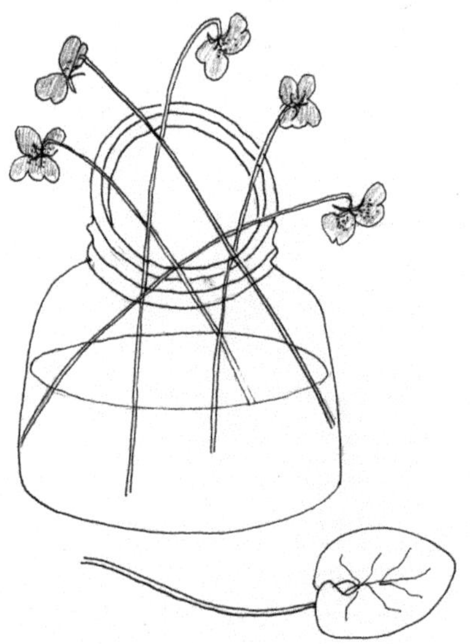

Think of a violet

Not of its stifled heart bellowing into blue
or of its deliquescence in the cold war of morning:
think of the fact of a violet.

Think of small hands parting the leaves to reach the stem,
thin as a promise,
ten times the resilience.

Think of small hands picking a violet,
then another and another.
Enough to engender hope – no, more.

Think of them carried in a jam jar down the long corridor,
water lapping up and over the rim,
the distillation of love.

Place them on the nightstand
beside an absence of roses,
a talisman for courage on the long journey home.

Help your son up onto the bed. Dry his hands with kisses.
Show him his sister there in the crib beneath the violets.
Think of the violets.

Corona radiata

My child's basket
is near to bursting,
the first egg ready to roll.
The bright blush of its demise
will trickle down the filtered lens
of her childhood,
pool in concavities
of that roller-coaster ride,
smear the fine crystal
of her laughter.

Like the pin-prick curse of Carabosse,
there'll be no turning back.
But by the grace of all that's good,
those first few eggs,
the corona radiata
patterned and scrolled
like a gypsy caravan,
will fall free
with the ease and equanimity
of her slow smile.

She just wants the first one
done with.

What's a tosser?

Mum, what's a tosser?
my teenage daughter asks,
looking up from her homework.

Well . . . Well it's a name you'd call
someone you didn't like, an insult.

But what does it actually mean?

A definition. Right. Well, I guess a tosser
is . . . is someone who plays with their
genitals . . . someone who mastur . . . who . . .
What subject is this anyway?

Netball, she replies.

Large

I'm going shopping, I said to my son.
Is there anything you need?
Yes, he said. *Condoms.*
Oh, I said. Condoms. Any particular sort?
Yes, he said. *Large.*
Large, I said. Just 'large'? Is there no particular colour you fancy?
No thanks. Just large.
What about flavour? I asked. Peppermint, raspberry, bubble gum?
No thanks Mum. Large will be fine.
Glow-in-the-dark perhaps? I hear they're lots of fun.
No Mum. Large.
Not even ribbed ticklers? I said. They're all the rage these days.
Mum, he said. *They don't even make large ones with all that other stuff.*
Don't they? I said. Why not?
Because if you're large, you don't need anything else do you?

I smiled all the way to the supermarket.
My son. Large.

I could say I was tickled pink.
But perhaps I should settle for proud.
Very, very proud.

The gift you give yourself

At the end of another Christmas Day
alone at last, secluded,
may all your Christmases come at once –
may batteries be included.

Puppetry of the penis

As little boys in a tent on the back lawn at midnight,
they amused themselves with hand puppetry:
Here is a rabbit, here is a butterfly, here is Optimus Prime
under attack from the Evil Decepticons.

Now grown men, naked in a spotlight before eight hundred people,
they amuse others with the Ancient Art of Genital Origami:
Here is the Sydney Harbour Bridge, here is the Eiffel Tower,
here is the Loch Ness monster.

Before each new creation – *Wrist Watch, Windsurfer, the Wind Up* –
they take their apparatus and rub and roll it
as though it were putty,
the pink plasticine of kindergarten playrooms.

One day, they'll turn it to its true purpose,
and father the next generation of little boys in backyard tents.
Later still, in the nursing home, their once-fêted
Leaning Towers of Pisa in a permanent state of collapse,

they'll sit round a table in the activities room
and with little squares of coloured paper
and diminished supplies of dexterity and patience,
fold another crane for Hiroshima Day.

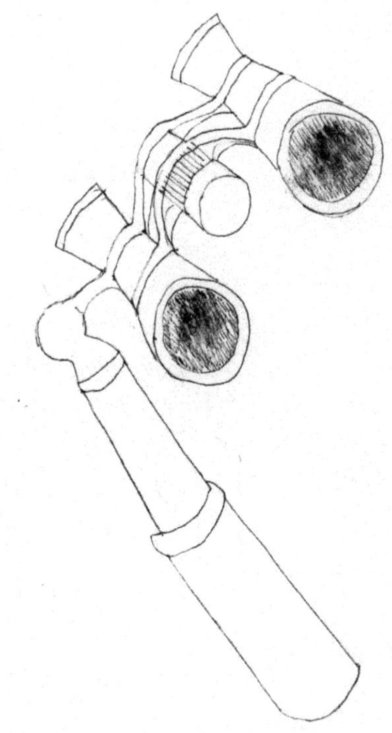

First Penis Transplant

cutting from 'The Sydney Morning Herald', 2106

Today, the first penis transplant was successfully performed on a woman in her twenties. *I've always wanted one,* stated the Sydney housewife, *to prove that women can wear penises too. I don't intend to flash it nor thrash it, just use it for its natural purposes and I hope it comes in handy around the house. I want to invent practical attachments such as dusters and dish mops. How many mothers have wished for an extra hand? – Crossing the street with a child each side, I'll hang my handbag on nature's hook. And when I go dancing on summer nights, I'll wear bangles that jangle from side to side. I really think they're going to catch on. Women have been without them far too long.* Surgeons say their lists are full of women waiting to fulfil their masculinity; the problem at the moment, it seems, lies in the distinct lack of donors.

Silly mid-on

If I composed a sonnet just for you
with ten syllables gracing every line
and not one beat too many or too few
and at the end of each a word to rhyme
with another lower down – look, see it?
would I, compared to One Day Cricket, say,
bowl your heart clean over? Would you deem it
'Stumps' perhaps, and skip the instant replay?
That is, of course, if I could shift your gaze
from silly mid-on long enough to read
said sonnet, and then (oh happy days!)
if with a nod you smilingly decreed,
'It seems Warne's place is not unfillable –
but check 'three up'; you're short one syllable.'

Her summer feet

A rainstorm is tearing at gum trees,
spiralling down leaves, fountaining
over gutters, and she's on the front veranda,
shoes off, skating on the smooth cement.

When the rain has eased, she's checking
her rubber boots for cobwebs, then marching
along rows of agapanthus, cracking and squashing
the round brown humps of emerging snails.

And when the steam rises with the sun,
she dons her thongs, searches the nasturtium patch
for silver beads, rolling like mercury on round leaves.
Laps each one up like a thirsty lizard.

Chance meeting

He'd made a camp of branch and canvas
among the acacias on the river bend,
forked fishing posts leaning to and fro.
The sand is fine and grey like the curls
massed wet on his dark forehead.
He tells me the fish are asleep now
and we must wait until sundown
– then I'd better be quicker than he.
A mile of white teeth spans his cheeks
his brow creases like the striations
in these Murray cliffs.

The trunk of the river red gum is plump
and knotted, and bears the marks of steps.
He directs my eyes upward to a long
vulva-shaped scar. Here a canoe was born,
he tells: his own grandfather cut the wood
with sharpened flint, and launched it
there where sand meets twisted roots.
His voice is river-slow and soft
as he wishes me luck on my trip.
My tinny tackle-box rattles away.
The scream of my outboard obscene.

Blue movie

Worldwide, the sea
draws bare skin to its sandy dress circle,
swallows the eyes
of mankind. We stand and stare out
at the flickering screen
while a thousand silver memories dart
like schools of fish.

In this matinee with sad gulls shrilling
and a blue boat
pulling on its anchor rope, the sun massages
my body, my soul
as I breathe in the whole seductive scene.
Fingering a pebble
and a pink cockle, I take part of it home
in my pocket.

The loquat tree

I had to beat the birds to win the fruit,
although half the delight was afterwards,
in the sucking of those perfectly rounded
brown seeds. Hard-earned, exotic,
like a Bedouin bride followed through a dry year
then wed when ripe with veiled secrets.
The best flesh is firm, skin golden,
scent verging on drunken.

I always strive for the tallest,
yellowest limb. The rasp of harsh leaves
won't stop me undressing a perfect clump.
Black twigs may fall in my eyes,
jealous birds might dive but when
I have a chance at kissing the Bedouin bride,
it's worth every trial, every stained shirt
for that luscious chin-drip.

Magpies

In the deserted schoolyard, a baby magpie stands its ground
squawks the squawk of a two year-old's tantrum.
Its mother on fast-forward –
Charlie Chaplin in a bakery at lunchtime –
darts across the asphalt and returns with a vegemite crust.

She drops it into the gaping maw of cacophony,
and with the faith of a committed Darwinian
that half empty will one day register as half full,
stands back and listens for the slightest turn
in the evolutionary wheel. Forsaken again, she races away

returns with a sultana plucked from the corpse
of a buttered bun, the thin edge of a pie crust –
anything to stop the din and hear instead the wind
in the tree-tops, a fluting call, tidings from the clan
gathering for evensong down at the river's edge.

Two streets away, outside the Country Bakehouse,
a child's newfound will, his mother's determined won't,
entertain the passers-by. The town matrons swoop in,
turn away from flailing arms, feed one another declarations
of the lack of discipline, the need for a 'good smack'.

But in the schoolyard, there's only me
and I'm on the side of this put-upon mother
who must restore peace
with little more than instinct,
and both hands tied behind her back.

Con nubial

What is it that calls them like lemmings
to churches and gardens, those precipices in waiting?
Is it the frothy sea of chiffon and tulle;
the waving crowds, smiling with hope and pity?

Will you take this seething rod of jealousy
to be a staff for your open wounds?
Will you promise to feed it, clothe it
and lick the salt from between its toes?

Will you take this bombshell of gristle and hair
set to explode your solitude?
Will you promise to light marital pyres
with your burning sulking silence?

And, will you both vow not to bolt or bite
through sickness and in health, while you
are whipped and tamed and made to perform,
daily, in the matrimonial circus?

Somnambulist

She trails her sculptured sheet to a
misty window
warmth falling away like layers of
skin.
The cold invades the folds of
flannelette.
The island bed sinks away
in shadow.
The glass is icy on her fingertips as she
wipes
a peep hole, a telescope to see him
leave
through the long soft tunnel
of morning.
A final glimpse of his black hair,
his long coat,
before his car coughs and
wakes her.

A little night music

Once, he'd lean over to her side of the bed
stroke the soft white of her inner thigh
until they began slow dancing –
that tight contrapuntal duet as the pulse
of a bow vibrates deep and low
in the bellies of two finely-tuned cellos.

Now, there are times he's lying
on top, emptying his testes and
it's just sex, not making love and she knows
it's a selfish thing this rubbing and jerking.
She could be a lump of meat or a handful of Ponds.
She turns her head to the side and thinks of
her mother and all her grandmothers and somehow
there are worse positions to be in, and there are better.

The pill is her modern right but orgasm is still hard won.
It's a bonus if she hits the jackpot
when he's only playing one line. She waits for the
final crescendo from this grunting tuba with an elbow
on her shoulder and a wad stuck in the funnel.

Waste

I line the kitty-litter tray
with faces of brides and grooms
smiling from Sunday's news.
Being a recent divorcee,
it says it all really.

Villanelle for a late husband

'You know you're just a jealous bitch,' he said,
'There's not a drop of perfume on my shirt!
I'm sorry babe, it's all inside your head,
so take a sleeping pill and go to bed.'

His patronising put-downs stabbed and hurt.
'You know you're just a jealous bitch,' he said.

You promised to be faithful when we wed.
You're out all night, you treat me just like dirt.
'I told you babe, it's all inside your head.'
So what about this earring in our bed?
This photo of some mini-skirted tart?

'You know you're just a jealous bitch,' he said,
'You're fat and boring and your eyes are dead.'
You cheater, you will pay for this, I spat.
'Sorry babe, it's all inside your head'.

An axe blade through his forehead. How he bled.
It drowned the scent of Chanel on his shirt.

Oh, yes, I'm just a jealous bitch, I said.
So sorry Babe, it's all inside your head!

Breakfast

Today, when I sat down to my morning egg,
severed its egg-y head,
scooped out its egg-y brains,
mashed them till they bled,
spread them on a pyre of burnt toast
and ate the egg-ing things . . .

I hardly thought of you at all.

Animi causa

Blessed are the celibate for they
shall inherit their due pleasures
without incurring bodily taxes,
without martyring themselves
to the twisted beliefs of the masses.

May their bodies writhe and shine,
mouths utter mantras of shameless beauty,
may they wear no lover's ring
nor vow nor bow, but stand reverent,
fingers curled in a labour of love.

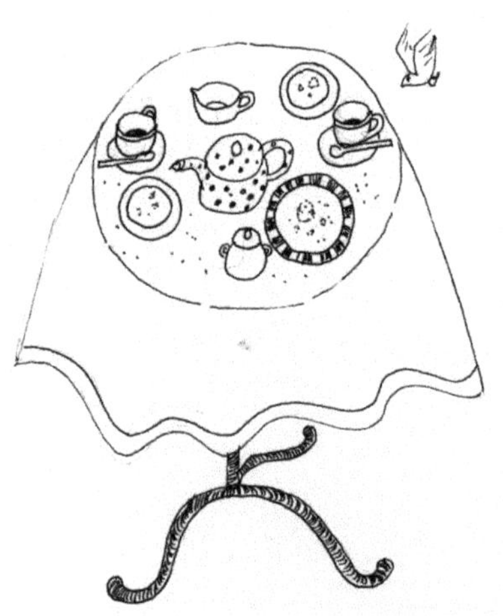

Bird at *The Edge*

Into the labyrinthine dip and curl
of our coffee-shop conversation –
your philandering husband, my senescent mother,
the high price of housing, the low line of televangelism –

comes a sparrow
that hops at the edge of our despair
until it charms an opening, a parting of the waters,
then taking its fill of pear and ginger cake-crumbs,

flies away,
and returns with the gift of single feather,
as though to remind us that sometimes
what goes around comes around by the very next post

and that even the marketing crassness
of, 'Buy Jesus, get Moses free!'
can shed a little lightness of being
on this otherwise deluded and doltish Sunday.

Knifing the ice

I forced the Simpson to abdicate.
Switched off from duty,
its empire crumbles to my deft blade.
Marble-white ruins fill my sink.
Bread tags float like the Armada.

For three generations
women have performed the ritual,
endured the smarting pain
to rid the fridge of its lining.
More than nine months
since I last padded the floor
with old towels
and waited for the trickle.

Tonight, I feast
on defrosted food
to celebrate kitchen victory,
a new cycle.

Pressing thoughts

She knows her clients by aroma.
Their hot essences penetrate her senses
like a lover's tongue.
Musk from the underwear of muscular Mr R,
patchouli in the sleeves of Bohemian Miss M,
and how did Mr T lose that trouser button?
She imagines them in creaseless garments
at parties and secret rendezvous.

Steam enhances her day dreams,
fabric patterns mingle
with the scent of humanity.
Her hands work automatically,
slick fingers always outrunning
the scorching tip of her tool.

Ironing is like love, she thinks.
You get burnt until you're experienced.
Then it's warm and heady
especially on cold afternoons
when a Hawaiian shirt with hot Brut
yachts you to the Caribbean.

Blow-dried

I like this crew of third-generation Port Adelaide barbers.
They plumb a line of integrity clear through to sailing ships
placing their faith in a compass and the steadfastness of stars.
Oh, they'll quiff and curl if that's your whim;
take two and a half hours and the down payment
on your island cruise to give you the latest look –
the one part wind, two parts terror
of the crow's-nest novice on the *Mary Celeste*.
But if you give them their head – and yours –
they'll navigate by the stars again,
feel their way through your locks
to find the well-spring of that natural wave,
the kiss that curls at the nape of your neck,
the true expression of your soul.
See? Just to my left, the blonded tips
of the Flicked-up Neophyte; to my far right,
the short back and sides of the Age-old Luddite.

And directly in front is a fifty-two-year-old Born-again Virgin,
utterly becalmed and not so much as an island in sight.
If only they'd learn to lie a little.

The downstairs maid

after The Sonnet, a painting by George Washington Lambert (1873–1930)

On a backdrop of tussocked hills and autumn sky,
he placed a man and a woman,
rugged them up in coats and hats.
Then seeing how palpable the silence between them
gave the man a book of sonnets,
the woman an attentive ear,
albeit hidden beneath a dark sweep of hair.

Next morning,
from beyond the rim of a chipped teacup,
he saw the silence had returned.
Saw how it trounced the words of the sonnet
as they limped and bleated from the man's mouth,
watched as it wallowed in a rising tide
of the woman's indifference.
He set the cup aside and with a brush plucked
from the bitter pool of experience,
between the man and the woman,
he juxtaposed a nude.

Tactful admirers averted their gaze,
spoke of allegory, a metaphysical construct,
fanned into flame by the words of the sonnet.
Only he saw the light slip from her shoulders,
catch in the nuzzle of breast and arm.
Only he knew the man had revised his choice of sonnet.
Only he knew the one he chose – chapter, line and parody:
Shall I compare thee to the downstairs maid?

Isabella and the pot of basil: The nurse's story

after a tale from Boccaccio and a poem by Keats

1.

When we came upon that place – chestnut casings sharp beneath our feet,
chapel bells bruising the morning air, the red berries of a whortleberry
    bush –
she flung herself down and wailing a noose around my heart
scraped and clawed at the fresh-thrown earth.
Then, wailing still but softly now as though she feared to wake him,
she pushed the loam from Lorenzo's brow, his unseeing eyes,
the cleft of his chin. She bent and pressed her lips to the chill of his,
and as her long hair settled about him like a shroud,
I remembered that night in mid-July, the light of day still searing the sky,
when I spied them beneath a garden bower – he, gazing up at her
as though she held the wonders of a comet blazing across the heavens;
she, moving above him, a pendulous blossom blown by summer breezes.
So when she asked for the blade, the one she had told me to secrete within
    my sleeve,
I knew and did not know what she intended, and refused. Then, seeing
    how thin
the thread that tethered her mind, and glad of a steel so recently sharpened,
I, her nurse since childhood, knelt beside her, an accomplice.

2.

In a garden pot beside her bed the basil bush flourished like none I'd seen.
Some thought it the perfumed liniments she plied as to a wound
that brought such lushness to its leaves and more fragrance to the touch
than ever cook could coax from her spindly kitchen plant.
Only I saw the lank strands of her hair entwine with the foliage
as she pressed her fevered lips to each newborn leaf.
Only I saw her tears like pale berries from a whortleberry bush
fall upon the leaves, trickle down the stem and soak into the soil.
Only I knew of their meandering descent
through runnels of their own making,
to reach at last their mouldering quarry: veiled with her white silk scarf –
Lorenzo's brow, his unseeing eyes, the cleft of his chin.

Apartheid

Salisbury Airport, Rhodesia, 1972

In the forest of people waiting for their luggage
she is just another tree. Brown pants, brown shoes,
all but hidden beneath an oversized poncho,
she is dressed to un-impress.
Even the flame of hair, the flaunt of freckles
across her pale nose and cheeks, appear subdued.
Go about your business, she seems to say.
I am nobody. I am nothing. I am not here.

On the other side of the carousel he too
is just another tree. Tall, skin the colour
and gloss of burnt wood, he too has learned
the art of invisibility and slipped it on
over his usual flamboyance.
His thoughts have been carefully chosen
and neatly folded to fit snug
within the framework of his face.
Not one escapes. All borders are closed.
When he lights a cigarette he exhales
through the tight-lipped corner of his mouth.

She does not look at him.
He does not look at her.
Each is so obviously alone.

What made them think that they would not be noticed?
That love would not resist all their efforts to disguise it
and by the power invested in it
pronounce them 'Guilty'.

Circles of light

Hoarstones 1633

Through leaves, I see them lash the girls to boughs
set faggots like rosettes about their feet.
The men are gathering sticks from fields around
to place beneath each skirt for added heat.

I know that poor Morag was caught bare shinned
with a naked saddler who was not her brother.
Her husband tests a finger to the wind,
then he signs the cross. In hatred, I shudder.

Jennet was around when the lord's horse died.
He hit her breast and buttocks for breaking in.
'Damn you bitch to bite my hand!' he cried.
'You're a witch. A witch. I saw you fly on the wind!'

> *In this sacred spot*
> *I pledge myself to Shalag ag Nog.*
> *Tonight, two circles of light, the work of an evil god.*
> *Curse these men, they'll die like dogs.*

At rise of moon, the churchmen gather and wait
to pitch their poisoned words, torches alight.
My drumming heart threatens to give me away
perched in the fork of an oak, my leafy hide.

Circles of light 'round the trees. Flames
bare their thighs. Men feast on flesh denied.
I feel the heat. My skull is full of screams.
These devils will suffer for their accursed lies.

For I am the crone who lives with the birds in the woods
where roots and thickets hide my friends and me.
They'll come with swords and hounds, and they'll look
but won't find my brew of hemlock leaves.

On this sacred spot
I pledge my love to Shalag ag Nog.
Two circles of light tonight are the work of an evil god.
King James, your cursed men will writhe and die and rot.

Diary of a maid

Asia Minor

Today the sun was kind, the morning cloud severed by its radiance. Again I sewed for Judith widow of Bethulia, working my threads from the first blush of dawn to crepuscular vespers. The bodice is finished and hangs on a hook behind the door, the neckline dives deeper than any I have sewn before. As I fitted the lining of her skirt, a blackbird sang from a high bough and I blessed each stitch on these cumquat layers where already a sheath is concealed like a snake in autumn leaves . . . Tonight I heard the widow speaking to the spirits: 'Dear husband, give me strength,' she pleads. And when she visits me, she removes her widow's weeds, tries on the dress, parades before me with a face by turns humble, brave and terrified.

xxx xxx xxx

Tomorrow I will line the palm-rope basket, test it's strong enough to hold wine, roasted grain, a cornucopia of roots and fruits, all we have. I'm certain the basket will carry her quarry . . . I saw him once through a spy-hole in the wall which both protects and pens us in like animals for the slaughter. He smiled. I fled. I will pad the basket with powdered orris root to absorb any blood that may spill.

xxx xxx xxx

A New Moon last night blessed our return. At sunrise, the Assyrian army fled when they found Holofernes felled like a giant palm tree, a necklace of red around his headless trunk. And after we rested, Judith told me that his face changed from lust to astonishment as it rolled.

xxx xxx xxx

The Sabbath. After thirty-four days, a stream of dusty people poured through the gates to celebrate freedom gained, fields reclaimed. They drank like beasts from the springs. Deep into the green well Judith threw the fiery dress, our work put to rest in quiet water. And Holoferne's skull lies inside my woven nest in a rocky crevice nine-hundred cubits west of Bethulia. Tomorrow I will begin a night-gown of gossamer blue for our saviour Judith of Judah so she may rise to the stars and sleep soundly again on the feathery down of the milky way.

Entering the centre

1.
I view Australia through sunglasses
and splattered insects, in a choice of frames:
wide screen or side window.

Angles of a shabby town prick the horizon.
A rusty shed leans. Hats and checked shirts
vaporise around a petrol pump.

A surreal Medusa seduces my eyes, as an orange
road train snakes beside the Devil's Marbles
with a forked cloud billowing in its wake.

In this Dali heat-haze nothing is permanent;
even those heads of stone will nod and shrink
as generations of dingoes slink back into sand.

2.
I ache as I leave the long day on the dashboard
mirrored in my lenses. I walk
with the setting sun to a moth-lit motel.

My ego is frayed as the wings on the sill.
A dull memory of day is printed on my starless eyes.
On a foam raft, I float in ripples of nothing.

Sleep is punctured with dreams of runaway trucks.
Restless and sweating, I sense a length of string
attaching me to tomorrow, winding me back to the city.

At last, the pull of a full moon through curtains
is enough to lift me high over red sand, tufted dunes,
pale ghost gums. No road, as I follow the dingo.

The list of last remaining

after Linda Pastan

From the list of last remaining,
I choose the silver coins of light
that fall through trees at the beginning of autumn
but I also choose shadow,
the imperviousness of things, forcing light
to find an opening, and giving us pattern.

I choose mangoes because they keep
their promise – their taste is every bit
as good as their fragrance.
And I choose them again for their stony hearts
that slip from our fingers, refuse to come clean,
save the best for themselves.

From the list of last remaining, I choose my children:
she, because there must be an elemental good in the world;
and he, because he explains nothing and omits little.
I choose laughter because it joins the dots,
allows us to find the sense in senseless,
connects us all to the last.

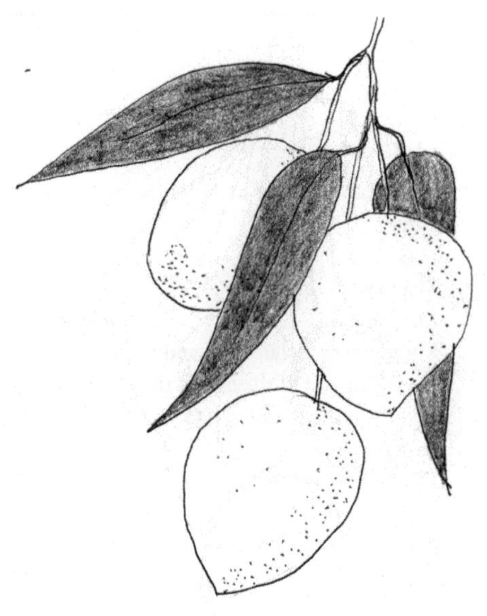

by Louise

by Jude

A little night music
Amnion
Animi causa
Beauty and the breast
Blue movie
Chance meeting
Circles of light
Con nubial
Delta nightclub
Diary of a maid
Entering the centre
First Penis Transplant
Fungi
Ghazal of the darkness
Grandmothers
Her summer feet
Knifing the ice
Nipples
Our short love
Pressing thoughts
Pantyhose
Phat is fat, however it's spelled
Power of attorney
Roll-ons
Somnambulist
Stone shoes
The call
The Head Mistress's speech
The loquat tree
Third trimester
Villanelle for a late husband
Visiting the room
Vulva speak
Waste
Weekly battle
What's a tosser?

Acknowledgements

Some of the poems in this collection have been published in the following anthologies and magazines: *Agenda* (UK), *Antipodes* (USA), *ArtState, Beyond the Shimmering, Blast, Blue Dog, Egg Poetry, Five Bells, Famous Reporter, Four W, Friendly Street readers, Frontier, Galloping On, Hobo, New England Review, On Dit, Page Seventeen, Pendulum, Poetrix, Poetry without Borders, Quadrant, Redoubt, Ripples, SideWalk, Short and Twisted, Southern Review, Studio, Tamba, The Best Australian Poems 2005* (Black Inc; Ed. Les Murray), *The Best Australian Poetry 2007* (UQP; Ed. John Tranter), *The Canberra Times, The Independent Weekly, Vibrant, Wet Ink.*

Our sincere thanks to all those who helped in the creation and production of this book. Special thanks to Rick Atkinson for his patience and brilliance in creating the illustrations throughout the book; to Jan Owen for expert advice during the editing of the poems; to Sue Elliot, and SA Cervix Screening for recognising the place that poetry can play in supporting women's health initiatives; Marg Davy (and her wit) for being the muse behind some of the women's health poems; Michael Bollen and the staff at Wakefield Press for ongoing publishing support; Arts SA for help with funding the WomanSpeak project; to Barbara Wiesner and all those at the SA Writers' Centre for their tireless support of South Australian writers; to Peter Bishop of Varuna Writers' House for his confidence in our collaboration and for offering us the Macquarie Bank Longlines Residency during which many of the poems were written; and last but never least our fellow poets, families and friends for reminding us of what's really important.

Louise Nicholas was born in Port Lincoln, South Australia. She has published a further seven collections of poetry. These include *The Red Shoes* (in Friendly Street Poets 'New Poets Three'), *The List of Last Remaining* (Five Islands Press), *Large* (Garron Press), *Meet My Mother* (Ginninderra Press), and three self-published chapbooks of humorous verse. Her work has been published in three *Best of Australian* . . . anthologies and she has been a guest speaker at many community events and festivals.

With a background that included Croatian, Scottish and English heritage, **Jude Aquilina** grew up in Magill, South Australia. She matriculated at Norwood High School and her early jobs included as a writer for Flim Flam Singing Telegrams and selling piano accordions. Jude's poetry and short stories are published across Australia and abroad. She has taught creative writing for three decades, at Flinders University, Adelaide College of the Arts, at libraries, schools, community centres and in a prison. Jude works as an educator, editor, writing mentor and is partner in Em-Dash Publishing. She has published four books with Wakefield Press including *Knifing the Ice*, *On a Moon Spiced Night* and *WomanSpeak* (with Louise Nicholas). Jude Aquilina lives in Milang and was the 2018 recipient of the Barbara Hanrahan Fellowship for her sustained contribution to South Australian literature.

Rick Atkinson lives in Adelaide where he was born in 1943. He spent a great deal of his life teaching architecture and urban design until recently, when he cut loose to find more diverse ways of pursuing his interest in urban life. The latest of these has been an invitation from Jude and Louise to sketch his responses to some of the poems in *WomanSpeak*. Rick still maintains his urban design teaching through annual design studios in both Adelaide and Penang.

Wakefield Press is an independent publishing and distribution company based in Adelaide, South Australia. We love good stories and publish beautiful books. To see our full range of books, please visit our website at www.wakefieldpress.com.au where all titles are available for purchase. To keep up with our latest releases and news, subscribe to the *Wakefield Weekly* at https://mailchi.mp/wakefieldpress/subscribe

Find us!

Facebook: www.facebook.com/wakefield.press
Instagram: www.instagram.com/wakefieldpress

www.ingramcontent.com/pod-product-compliance
Ingram Content Group Australia Pty Ltd
76 Discovery Rd, Dandenong South VIC 3175, AU
AUHW020208230226
423697AU00001B/9

9 781862 548473